7 YEARS

Words and Music by LUKAS FORCHHAMMER,
MORTEN RISTORP, STEFAN FORREST,
DAVID LABREL, CHRISTOPHER BROWN
and MORTEN PILEGAARD

PIANO · VOCAL · GUITAR

LUKAS GRAHAM

ISBN 978-1-4950-6542-2

7777 W. BLUEMOUND RD. P.O. BOX 13819 MILWAUKEE, WI 53213

In Australia Contact:
Hal Leonard Australia Pty. Ltd.
4 Lentara Court
Cheltenham, Victoria, 3192 Australia
Email: ausadmin@halleonard.com.au

Visit Hal Leonard Online at
www.halleonard.com

TAKE THE WORLD BY STORM

Words and Music by LUKAS FORCHHAMMER, STEFAN FORREST,
MORTEN RISTORP, DAVID LABREL, MORTEN PILEGAARD,
CHRISTOPHER BROWN and ROSS GOLAN

*Recorded a half-step higher

live and learn, don't mat-ter if I land or if____ I fall.____

____ I know I might re-turn, at least I know

I'll be walk-ing tall. I'm not a-fraid____

'cause I____ take the world by

MAMA SAID

Words and Music by LUKAS FORCHHAMMER, STEFAN FORREST,
MORTEN RISTORP, MORTEN PILEGAARD, CHRISTOPHER BROWN,
CHARLES STROUSE and MARTIN CHARNIN

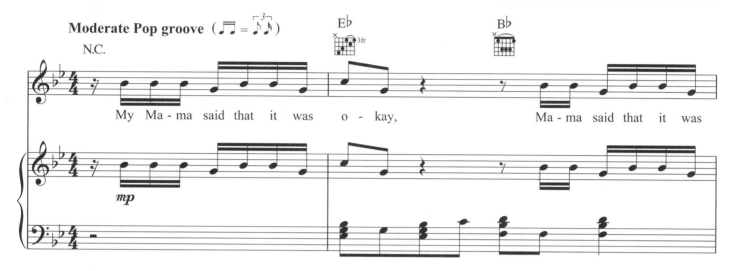

My Ma-ma said that it was o-kay, Ma-ma said that it was

quite al-right. Our kind of peo-ple had a bed for __ the night and it was o-kay.

Ma-ma told us we were good kids and Dad-dy told us, "Nev-er

Dm **Gm** **Dm** **Gm**

lis - ten to ___ the ones point-ing nas - ty fin-gers and mak - ing fun," 'cause we were good kids.

F **N.C.** **Gm** **F/A**

Re-mem-ber ask-ing both my mom and dad why we nev - er trav-eled to ex-
have it bad, I got e - nough lov-ing from my

B♭ **Gm** **F/A**

ot - ic lands. We on - ly ev - er real-ly vis - it friends, noth-ing to tell when the
mom and dad. But I don't think they real-ly un-der-stood when I said that I want-ed the deal in

B♭ **Gm** **E♭**

sum-mer ends. We nev - er real-ly went buy - ing clothes, folks were pass-ing on this stuff in
Hol - ly-wood. I told them I'll be sing-ing on T - V, the oth - er kids were call-ing me a

To Coda ⊕

lis-ten to ___ the ones   point-ing nas-ty   fin-gers and mak - ing fun,"   'cause we were good kids.

Don't get me wrong, I   did - n't

I know which   place I'm   from, _____   I   know   my   home.

When I'm   in doubt and   strug-gl - ing,   that's where I   go.   An old

HAPPY HOME

Words and Music by LUKAS FORCHHAMMER, STEFAN FORREST,
MORTEN RISTORP, DAVID LABREL, MORTEN PILEGAARD,
CHRISTOPHER BROWN, RASMUS HEDEGARD
and CHRISTIAN WORSOE

Steady half-time feel

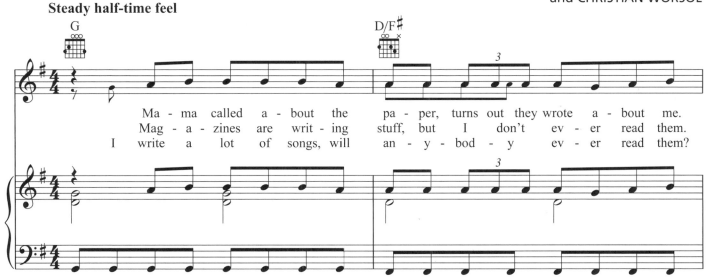

Ma-ma called a-bout the pa-per, turns out they wrote a-bout me.
Mag-a-zines are writ-ing stuff, but I don't ev-er read them.
I write a lot of songs, will an-y-bod-y ev-er read them?

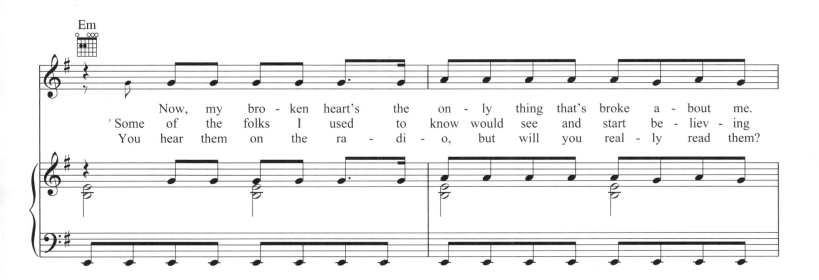

Now, my bro-ken heart's the on-ly thing that's broke a-bout me.
'Some of the folks I used to know would see and start be-liev-ing
You hear them on the ra-di-o, but will you real-ly read them?

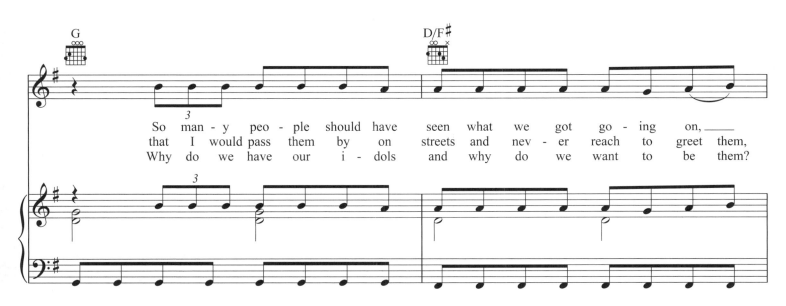

So man-y peo-ple should have seen what we got go-ing on,
that I would pass them by on streets and nev-er reach to greet them,
Why do we have our i-dols and why do we want to be them?

To Coda

Bm

I thought a - bout it for a while, and I'm at a loss.
it's al - right ___ now but what a - bout when I'm ___ old?
I still get ner - vous ev - 'ry time I know she's at a show.

Em

C

Know - ing that I'm gon - na live my ___ whole life with - out him,
I know my good friends, now they'll last.

D

Bm

I found out a lot of things I nev - er knew a - bout him.
The same ones that stood by me when my dad - dy passed. ___

Em

C

All I know is that I'll nev - er real - ly be a - lone
All I know is that we'll nev - er real - ly be a - lone

D

'cause we got a lot of love and a hap - py___ home.
'cause we got a lot of love and a hap - py___ home.

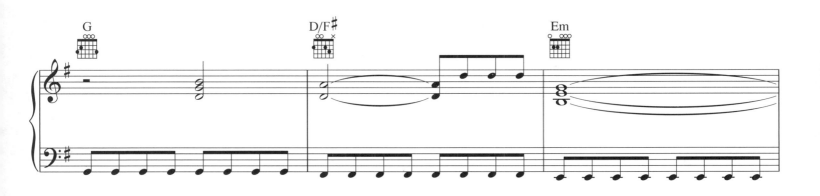

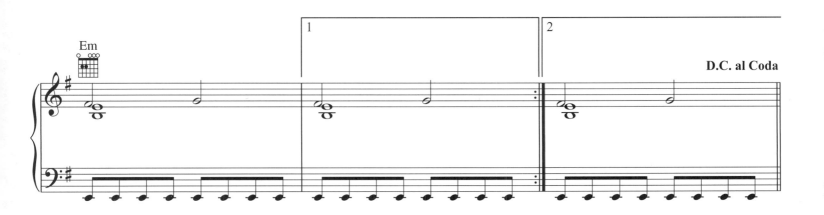

D.C. al Coda

DRUNK IN THE MORNING

Words and Music by LUKAS FORCHHAMMER,
STEFAN FORREST, MORTEN RISTORP, DAVID LABREL,
MORTEN PILEGAARD, CHRISTOPHER BROWN, SEBASTIAN FOGH,
MAGNUS LARSSON and MARK FALGREN

BETTER THAN YOURSELF
(Criminal Mind Pt. 2)

Words and Music by LUKAS FORCHHAMMER,
STEFAN FORREST, MORTEN RISTORP, BRANDON BEAL,
DAVID LABREL, MORTEN PILEGAARD, CHRISTOPHER BROWN,
RASMUS HEDEGARD and SEBASTIAN FOGH

hell. And there ain't, no, _____

no one can change it, no one can do it bet - ter than your - self.

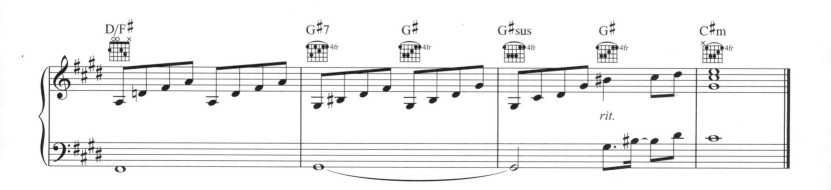

rit.

DON'T YOU WORRY 'BOUT ME

Words and Music by LUKAS FORCHHAMMER, STEFAN FORREST,
MORTEN RISTORP, DAVID LABREL, MORTEN PILEGAARD,
CHRISTOPHER BROWN and BRANDON BEAL

Gospel Soul

Hey, my friend, _ how you've been? What are you go - ing through? _

What is this trou - ble that's trou - bl - ing you? ___

WHAT HAPPENED TO PERFECT

Words and Music by LUKAS FORCHHAMMER, STEFAN FORREST,
MORTEN RISTORP, DAVID LABREL, MORTEN PILEGAARD,
CHRISTOPHER BROWN and ROSS GOLAN

STRIP NO MORE

Words and Music by LUKAS FORCHHAMMER, STEFAN FORREST,
MORTEN RISTORP, DAVID LABREL, MORTEN PILEGAARD,
CHRISTOPHER BROWN, SEBASTIAN FOGH, MAGNUS LARSSON,
MARK FALGREN and BRANDON BEAL

YOU'RE NOT THERE

Words and Music by LUKAS FORCHHAMMER, STEFAN FORREST,
MORTEN RISTORP, DAVID LABREL, MORTEN PILEGAARD,
CHRISTOPHER BROWN and JAMES GHALEB

FUNERAL

Words and Music by LUKAS FORCHHAMMER, STEFAN FORREST,
MORTEN RISTORP, DAVID LABREL, MORTEN PILEGAARD,
CHRISTOPHER BROWN and ROSS GOLAN